P9-CKK-716

Dear Parents and Educators,

Welcome to Penguin Young Readers! As parents and educators, you know that each child develops at his or her own pace—in terms of speech, critical thinking, and, of course, reading. Penguin Young Readers recognizes this fact. As a result, each Penguin Young Readers book is assigned a traditional easy-to-read level (1–4) as well as a Guided Reading Level (A–P). Both of these systems will help you choose the right book for your child. Please refer to the back of each book for specific leveling information. Penguin Young Readers features esteemed authors and illustrators, stories about favorite characters, fascinating nonfiction, and more!

Ocean Monsters

LEVEL 4

GUIDED READING LEVEL **N**

This book is perfect for a **Fluent Reader** who:
- can read the text quickly with minimal effort;
- has good comprehension skills;
- can self-correct (can recognize when something doesn't sound right); and
- can read aloud smoothly and with expression.

Here are some **activities** you can do during and after reading this book:
- Discuss: Voice is what gives writing personality, flavor, and style. Although this book is nonfiction and contains a lot of facts, the authors, Nick and Chelsea Confalone, have inserted their own voices to make the information more interesting to read. Instead of just listing dry facts, the authors make the readers feel as if they are talking to them about the most amazing creatures on Earth. One way Nick and Chelsea's voices come alive is through their use of story, such as the story of Mr. Picot's fight with the giant squid. Reread the book and discuss how Nick and Chelsea's voices make this nonfiction book more interesting to read.
- Research: Do your own research on one of the creatures in the book— the giant squid, the electric stargazer, the Japanese spider crab, the Portuguese man-of-war, the vampire squid, the deep-sea anglerfish, or the torpedo ray. What other facts can you find out?

Remember, sharing the love of reading with a child is the best gift you can give!

—Bonnie Bader, EdM
   Penguin Young Readers program

*Penguin Young Readers are leveled by independent reviewers applying the standards developed by Irene Fountas and Gay Su Pinnell in *Matching Books to Readers: Using Leveled Books in Guided Reading*, Heinemann, 1999.

To Leo, our favorite little monster—NC&CC

To my lovely and supportive wife,
Anastasia, and my two wonderful
daughters, Helen and Ellie—CR

PENGUIN YOUNG READERS
Published by the Penguin Group
Penguin Group (USA), 375 Hudson Street, New York, New York 10014, USA

USA | Canada | UK | Ireland | Australia | New Zealand | India | South Africa | China
Penguin Books Ltd, Registered Offices: 80 Strand, London WC2R 0RL, England

For more information about the Penguin Group visit penguin.com

Photo credits: page 13: (top and bottom) © Discovery Communications; page 15: © iStockphoto/
Thinkstock; page 17: © 2002–2013 Nature Picture Library; page 22: © iStockphoto/Thinkstock;
page 23: © Susan Dabritz/SeaPics.com; page 25: © MYN/Paul Marcellini/naturepl.com;
page 26: © David Fleetham/naturepl.com; page 27: © Thinkstock; page 30: © Thinkstock; page
34: © David Shale/naturepl.com; page 40: © David Shale/naturepl.com; page 44:
© Alex Mustard/naturepl.com; page 45: © Jose B. Ruiz/naturepl.com;
page 47: © Phillip Colla/SeaPics.com.

Text copyright © 2013 by Nick Confalone and Chelsea Confalone.
Illustrations copyright © 2013 by Penguin Group (USA). All rights reserved.
Published by Penguin Young Readers, an imprint of Penguin Group (USA),
345 Hudson Street, New York, New York 10014.
Manufactured in China.

Library of Congress Cataloging-in-Publication Data is available.

ISBN 978-0-448-46723-8 (pbk)   10 9 8 7 6 5 4 3 2 1
ISBN 978-0-448-46724-5 (hc)   10 9 8 7 6 5 4 3 2 1

Ocean Monsters

by Nick and Chelsea Confalone
illustrated by Chris Rallis and with photos

Penguin Young Readers
An Imprint of Penguin Group (USA)

Have you ever imagined creatures from another planet? Were they friendly? Were they scary? Do you search the stars night after night, hoping to catch a glimpse of something strange? Well, you can put your telescope away, because the strangest creatures of all live right here on planet Earth.

They do not live in deserts.

They do not live in jungles.

They do not live on mountains.

In fact, they do not live on land at all!

The strangest creatures on planet Earth live far, far below the surface of the sea.

Fish that use glowing "worms" for bait. Fish that zap their prey with electric shocks. Squid that glow in the dark. Crabs that are 12 feet long!

So put on your scuba gear and let's investigate these ocean monsters.

Giant Squid

October 25, 1873, started off as an
ordinary day for Mr. Picot. He got
into his boat and rowed out into the
waters off Bell Island, Canada, to fish.
Suddenly, he noticed something strange
floating in the water. Was it part of a
wrecked ship? A large sail? Mr. Picot
rowed closer. It looked like the top of a
mushroom, but it was almost the size of
his rowboat.

Then Mr. Picot thought he saw
the thing move! He was scared,
but he had to find out
what it was.

Mr. Picot rowed even closer. Carefully, he poked the thing with one of his oars. He heard a rumbling from deep within the ocean. His cold, wet fingers clutched the oar. His heart raced. He leaned out over the side of the boat. He squinted into the dark water.

This thing was 20 times bigger than he had thought it was!

Down below, he saw a giant eye looking back at him.

This thing was alive!

Smack! The bottom of Mr. Picot's boat shook. Water splashed up all around him. Tentacles (say: tent-TUH-kuhlz) rose out of the water. Everywhere he looked, Mr. Picot saw suction cups with sharp teeth. He tried to row away, but the tentacles grabbed his boat.

Water rushed over the side of the boat.
Quickly, Mr. Picot grabbed an ax.
He chopped off one of the giant
tentacles.

Fwoom! The monster sprayed black ink
all over the water. Ink covered the boat.
Ink covered Mr. Picot.

The monster swam away, leaving Mr. Picot alone and scared. He stared at the piece of tentacle that was in his hand.

Mr. Picot had just battled a **giant squid**. But not everyone believed his story. Some didn't even believe that the giant squid was real.

Over 100 years later, scientists finally were able to catch on camera a live giant squid, swimming in the ocean. It was nine feet long, but its two longest tentacles were missing. It is possible that with the tentacles, the squid might have been 26 feet long.

That might sound big, but the largest giant squid ever found measured 43 feet from its head to the tip of its tentacles. Its tentacles were lined with hundreds of suction cups, and each suction cup was filled with sharp teeth. Each eye was 10 inches in diameter (say: dahy-A-mi-ter). That's bigger than a bowling ball! This ocean monster weighed half a ton (that's 1,000 pounds!).

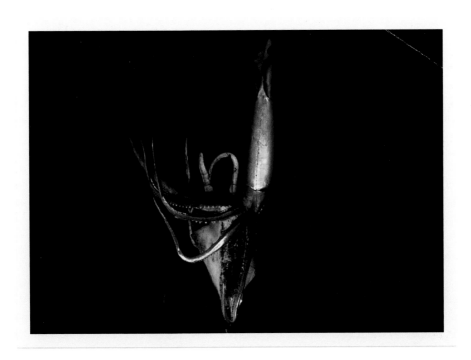

The giant squid eats fish that live deep in the ocean. Here comes one now. The giant squid floats far, far above the fish. *Snatch!* Its two extralong feeding tentacles shoot through the water and grab the fish from 40 feet away. The squid pulls the fish up to its beak. Its beak can bite through almost anything.

Chomp! It bites the fish. Now the water is filled with fish guts. Even the squid's tongue has tiny teeth on it. It licks the fish guts and shreds them into smaller pieces. Then—*gulp!*—the fish is gone.

ORANGE ROUGHY

Electric Stargazer

Life at the bottom of the ocean is cold, dark, and filled with predators. At least the sand is a safe place where nothing can eat you, right? Wrong!

A small fish swims above the sand. *Whoosh!* Something springs out—like a jack-in-the-box—and swallows the unlucky fish whole.

What is that thing that just sprang into action? It's the **electric stargazer**.

Stargazers are fish. They can be up to two feet long. Most of the stargazer's body hides under the sand. It is happy to lie there all day and wait and wait and wait. The stargazer knows that eventually a fish will swim by. And then it is suppertime!

ELECTRIC STARGAZER

17

This unlucky scuba diver reaches out to touch an electric stargazer. She sees that the stargazer has two poisonous (say: POI-zuh-nuhs) spines on its back. The diver is careful not to touch the spines, but the stargazer has a surprise for her. *Zap!* The stargazer shoots electricity out from right below its eyeballs. What in the world?!

Electric stargazers use electricity for self-defense. The scuba diver swims away. She won't be touching any more stargazers today.

Japanese Spider Crab

This crab is huge. Crabs found at the beach are usually no more than eight inches long. The **Japanese spider crab** has a leg span of 13 feet across! This huge monster of a crab can weigh up to 40 pounds. That is heavier than most three-year-old children.

0   1   2   3   4   5   6

The Japanese spider crab is an arthropod (say: AHR-thruh-pod). An arthropod is an animal that grows a superhard skeleton, called an exoskeleton (say: ek-soh-SKEL-eh-ten), on the outside of its body. Bees, ants, spiders, and crabs are all arthropods.

But the Japanese spider crab is the largest arthropod in the world.

7   8   9   10   11   12   13

Japanese spider crabs are scavengers.
They scuttle around on the ocean floor,
searching for food. Look, a rotten, dead
fish! To a spider crab, this dead body
will make a delicious meal. The crab
uses its pincers (say: PIN-serz) to grab
the decaying fish. Then the crab nibbles
until the fish is gone.

What else does a Japanese spider crab eat? Its own body! The spider crab's exoskeleton is made of chitin (say: KAHY-tin). Chitin is hard and strong, like a shell. As a spider crab grows, it sheds its exoskeleton and grows a new, bigger one. After the spider crab crawls out of its old exoskeleton, it turns around and eats it! It's disgusting, but that's the life of a scavenger.

EXOSKELETON

Portuguese Man-of-War

The **Portuguese man-of-war** looks like a giant jellyfish. It is not. The man-of-war is a collection of zooids. Zooids are individual animals that live together. They cannot survive on their own, so instead they act like one big animal. When the zooids work together as a Portuguese man-of-war, they are one of the most dangerous monsters in the ocean.

The Portuguese man-of-war got its name because sailors thought the crest looked like the sails of an old warship. It actually looks more like a gooey blob of tentacles, but sailors used their imaginations on those long, boring voyages. In any case, the name stuck.

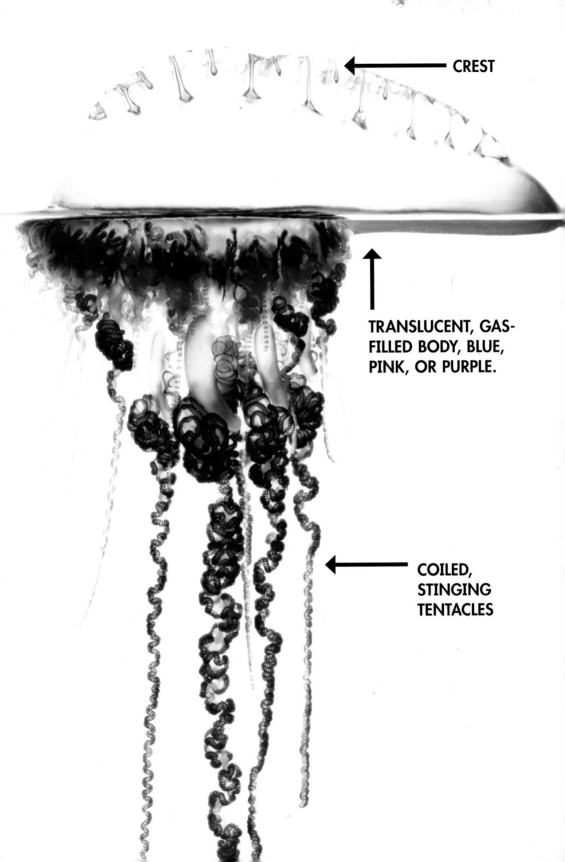

CREST

TRANSLUCENT, GAS-FILLED BODY, BLUE, PINK, OR PURPLE.

COILED, STINGING TENTACLES

The man-of-war has no way to move around on its own. It is happy to just float on warm ocean currents.

It is very large, and its sting is very strong. The man-of-war can eat whatever it wants and sting whatever gets in its way.

This clever fish thinks that it can outsmart the man-of-war. It swims far, far below it. But the man-of-war has tentacles that can be as long as 160 feet. That's longer than four school buses. Nice try, clever fish, but *snatch!*

160 FEET

Tentacles sting the fish and paralyze it with powerful venom. The tentacles pull the fish up. The fish tries to wiggle away, but its muscles won't move. The fish is pulled all the way up to the top of the man-of-war, where the man-of-war soaks it in special chemicals. The fish's skin melts. Then its face and bones melt, too. Soon there is nothing left of the fish but blood and gunk. But that's just how the man-of-war likes its dinner. *Slurp!*

Vampire Squid

In 1903, a German marine biologist named Dr. Carl Chun was hoping to discover new animals. He thought a good place to look was the deep, dark ocean. He sailed around the west coast of Africa, exploring the Guinea basin.

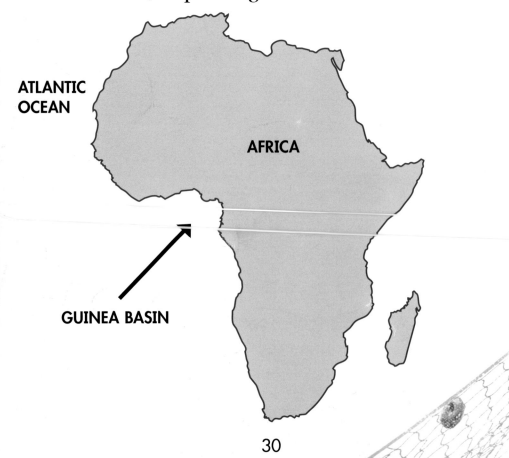

ATLANTIC OCEAN

AFRICA

GUINEA BASIN

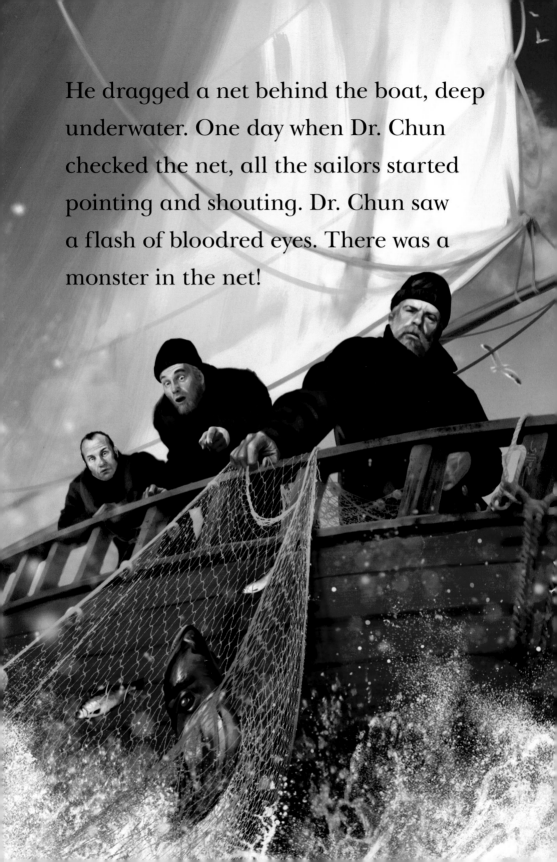

He dragged a net behind the boat, deep
underwater. One day when Dr. Chun
checked the net, all the sailors started
pointing and shouting. Dr. Chun saw
a flash of bloodred eyes. There was a
monster in the net!

It looked like it was hiding behind a cape—a cape made of skin. He called this monster the **vampire squid**.

The vampire squid has the biggest eyes for its size in the entire animal kingdom. Its deep-set eyes, which can be blue or red, are one inch across. That might not sound very big, but its body is only six inches around.

The vampire squid has eight tentacles and two filaments, which work like sensors. The tentacles are covered in spikes, and some have suction cups. All the tentacles are connected by a thin web of skin that looks like a cape.

Fwoosh! A hungry sea lion holds its breath and dives deep underwater. It sees a vampire squid up near the surface. A perfect lunch! But not so fast: The vampire squid folds its tentacles up over its head. Its webbing turns inside out.

Now the vampire squid looks like a
ball covered with spikes. Not so delicious
anymore, but the sea lion doesn't give
up. *Flash!* The vampire squid blinds the
sea lion with a burst of bright light. The
sea lion sees glowing spots and gets
confused. Then suddenly . . . darkness.
Where did the squid go?

The vampire squid has spots called photophores (say: FOH-tuh-fawrz) all over its body. Photophores are made of special chemicals that glow in the dark. They are like built-in flashlights. When the vampire squid wants to be sneaky, it turns off all the lights on its body. It disappears.

The sea lion searches the water. Suddenly it sees the outline of the squid! *Sploosh!* The vampire squid squirts out a thick blob of glowing mucus (say: MEW-kuhs) from the tips of its tentacles. Yuck!

The squid finally makes its escape. It leaves the sea lion covered in gross mucus.

Deep-Sea Anglerfish

At 3,000 feet below the surface, there is no light at all. Fish must hunt for food in the dark.

Fish get excited when they see a yummy little glow-in-the-dark worm! What a perfect snack! But watch out— it's a trick to lure small fish into the waiting jaws of the **deep-sea anglerfish**.

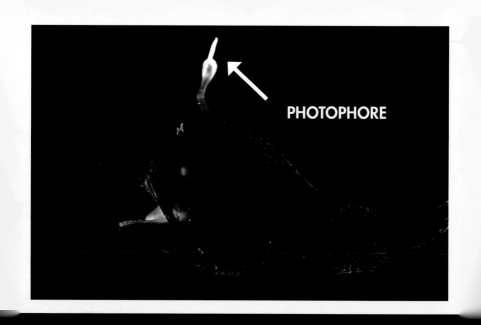

PHOTOPHORE

The anglerfish is almost invisible in the dark. It has thin skin that is slimy like jelly. Most are about the size of a basketball, but some deep-sea anglerfish can reach over three feet and weigh over 100 pounds. The sneaky anglerfish has a glow-in-the-dark photophore similar to the vampire squid. But the anglerfish's photophore is on a piece of spine that hangs over its mouth like a fishing pole with a worm hooked on the end.

Here comes a big fish, excited to check out the cool, glowing light. The anglerfish gets ready for dinner. But how can the small anglerfish fit the bigger fish into its mouth?

The anglerfish expands its stomach. Its jaws open wider and wider. Now its mouth is twice as big as before.

Chomp! The fish tries to escape. But the anglerfish has over 60 teeth, as sharp as razor blades. And the anglerfish's teeth point inward. The crooked teeth make it easy for fish to slide into the anglerfish's mouth. But what happens when the fish tries to escape? The inward-facing teeth shred the fish like confetti. The anglerfish eats the bloody mess in one giant swallow. *Gulp!*

Torpedo Ray

When navy submarines want to blow something up, they fire a torpedo (say: tor-PEE-doh). *Boom!* Did you know that the US Navy named their powerful weapon after a powerful stingray called the **torpedo ray**?

The torpedo ray looks kind of like a big pancake, about the size of a hula hoop, with a tail fin in the back. It does not hunt by chasing its prey. Instead, it lies flat on the ocean floor and waits and waits and waits. The torpedo ray doesn't have very good vision. It can't see a fish swimming right above it. But the torpedo ray is able to sense the electrical charges of the fish, so it knows that it's there.

Whoosh! The hungry torpedo ray darts off the ocean floor and curls up around the fish.

The fish is trapped by the torpedo ray. And then, *zap*! The fish feels like it's on fire. *Zap*! Every muscle in its body clenches at once. *Zap*! Its heart stops. The fish is dead. What happened?

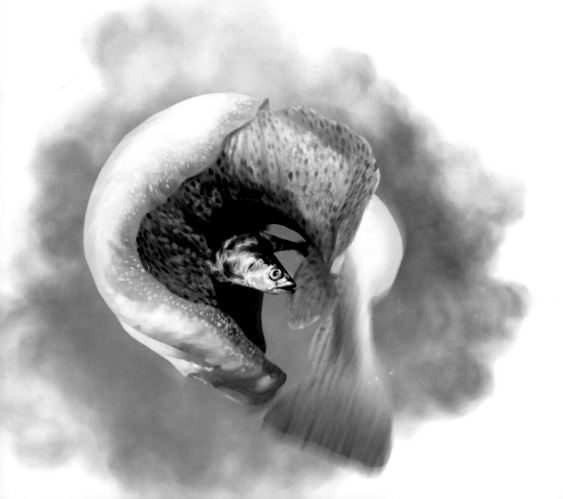

Torpedo rays can make electricity. They zap their prey with 220 volts. That's twice as much electricity as an outlet in a house. When it's finally time to eat the fish, torpedo rays take their time. They let go, turn the fish around, and eat it headfirst. *Crunch!*

New ocean monsters are being discovered all the time. Less than 5 percent of the world's oceans have been explored.

That means that 95 percent of what lies beneath the surface has not been seen yet by human eyes.

Who knows? Maybe you will be the one to discover the next ocean monster!